Jovi.Love

Javonna Wylie

BookLeaf Publishing

India | USA | UK

Presentation by *BookLeaf Publishing*

Web: www.bookleafpub.com

E-mail: info@bookleafpub.com

ISBN: 9789357445696

First edition 2022

DEDICATION

I dedicate this book to my baby sister Jai Jai. I pray you always know that I give my best to you and want nothing short of God's will and blessings for you. You are a walking miracle, manifested by love and grace and you should know this. All your dreams are achievable, beauty.

ACKNOWLEDGEMENT

I would like to acknowledge my best friend Chelle Victorya for introducing me to this publishing opportunity. I would like to acknowledge Varquidia for always encouraging me to write and publicize my work. I would like to thank Tay for the concept of Jovi.Love as Tay often knows me deeper than I know myself and would do anything to see me succeed. I would like to thank Qur'an for being one of the most extraordinary and enduring loves and friends I've ever known. I would like to acknowledge my Nana and Mom Mom for being my biggest confidants in life. Thank you to my family for unconditional love and support. Lastly, thank you to all my friends- close, near, far and via media because your support means the world to me. Thank you for seeing me.

PREFACE

If you know me in real life, you know my mind is a wild beautiful place. Thank you for being here, on this road with me as we travel down a new journey of publicity. Welcome to an expressway of love, being and possibly humor if we're in the same lane.

Jovi Love

The goal is to... truly spend time with myself.
Spend time with myself so that I can rediscover
what it truly means to be Jovi. I want to look in
the mirror and say "I love you" and mean it.
I want to mean it in the most holistic, pure way;
I want it to be one of the deepest and truest loves
that I've ever spoken in my entire being. I want
love to be my essence. But first,
I must be.
Beloved.
Be loved.
Be love.
Be, love.

Touchy Topic

Nothing made me feel alive anymore.
I asked God, "What do I need to do, God? What
do I need to do to trust you? What do I need to
do to be jovial again?"

He said: See that limb over there?
I said: Yes
He said: How would you categorize it?
I said: Categorize?
He said: Adjective. Big, ambiguous, small...
I said: That limb is little
God said: well that's your opportunity to a new
you. I need all 289lbs of you to faithfully and
courageously walk on that little limb. That's
where you'll find JoviAl.

A Stitch is Always Deeper Than It Seams

A stitch is always deeper than it seems. So a stitch may look like it has a couple loose ends but in reality we don't know the quality of that stitch, where it was imported from, how deep that stitch is and how long it took to get it that way, we don't know how many times it was washed, dried, left outside, brought back to life. I think it's okay to use our discernment when it comes to people of course; what's for us is for us. But as far as judgement, that's for the universe, God, karma to handle. So a lot of times I am iffy about judgement and I am iffy about title. If I had to pick a title that is fitting for me, it would be jovial. Because through every up and down, I am always jovial. Jovi The Modest.

imhotep

i bring the peace baby im hotep
i'm a lover and learner of life, im polymath
yall shady like this earth
i'm hip like these curves
i'm limitless like infinity or heaven or energy
Friends with all my "enemies"
I'm not from here; I'm a Martian
I'm from mars
I'm Javonna
But you can call me Jovi with the barz

Hu m i

I make up my mind about who I am everyday and then I remind myself of who I am every moment; if I don't make up my mind about me, there is a whole world that is waiting and ready to define me. -Javonna

Conju gyal

I wonder if it'll be like ecstasy
Having you next to me
Will a star burst
When we speak our first words
In person
Will you be thirsting?
Like all the men I've met over the years
Or will you be near tears
Because you've yearned
For this moment
For so long
Idk, prolong
I'm having all these jovi thoughts like
Does he floss his teeth?
Is it soft or scruffy, his taco meat?
Is he circumcised?
Does he ugly cry?
if he doesn't accept my free spirit
Do he know what that means? Does he
recognize?
When he grabs my arm, will there be butterflies?
I hope this trip is everything I could've dreamed
on and more
Sometimes you just have to trust God

WORM

I collect memories
Like damaged men collect thotties
Like dope boys collect bodies
Scotty Too Hotty

Butterfly

trying to play jov
is like inducing ur own coma
now ur on a gurney
prayers to you, babe
God bless ur journey
ur karma
got u wrestling internally
but like pac said
life goes on
so so long

dating in pennsylvania
it's like i'm always on the next season of
wrestlemania
i be on my scotty 2 hotty
cuz a shorty too popping
popping out
like a cacoon
now, boom
bish
i'm a butterfly

Solitude n all

Until you can look at my booty then witness my brokenness and still see my beauty, I don't have eyes for you, King.
Ask me what I've endured.
You gotta be someone I want my son to look up to.
You gotta be an example to my daughter and my sister and my God child.
I gotta know that you have not only the ability but the will to love me a billion years over.
And your soul... what's the condition of it?
Do you love yourself enough to let go of your ego?
Do you care for those less fortunate as much as I do?
Do you respect that Ima grind everyday, sometimes selflessly?
Do you suffer from jealousy?
Are you patient enough to respect celibacy, if I so choose?
No you're not perfect but do you have what it takes to Love a Queen?

Ask yourself that before you approach my
throne. I been through it all, if I can't have
Agape, trust me, I'm cool on my own

I am Whole-ish

People go through shit and never talk about it.
They think somehow bottling things up makes it
go away; creating their own life sentence. But
my motto is to never let my struggles be a
run-on. I put a period on every [life] sentence.
Then I express it...sometimes in poem or spoken
word or within day to day relationships. I write
my own story. I can't control everything that
happens to me. I cannot control when one that I
love or trust betrays me. I cannot control when
opportunity does not work in my favor. I cannot
control all of my circumstances---however I can
control how I feel about it ALL. I expose myself
to myself and reveal to others what I've endured
periodically. This is my strength. This is what
makes me Me. Everybody puts the Come Up on
display. They never talk about the hard work,
heart break, pain or defeat that propels them.
Impact.
I let my pain propel my purpose...and for that I
am whole

Jovi Adina

I admit that the freak in me puts it down but
I don't want just another encounter
I like... my hair gripped
Neck choked
Hard thrust up on the counter
Top
But
Even more so
I like long walks
And deep talks
And to share the same towel
Because your natural scent is just that appealing
to me
I like feelings and shit
And when tough times come I like to deal with it
Because I value truth
And transparency
When you tell me you fucks with me Ima be
right at you with the questions liiiiike "okay,
come sit ya ass right here and let's see"
I want to express all my ideas with someone
You got me wine and flowers?
Bet forget the outing, let's just kickback and
watch Power

I like adventures and making silly videos and
#CoupleShit
And someone who has respect for women
Not just the one that he's dealing with
A
Soul
That loves old school hip hop and R&B
And you better turn up with me when the DJ
drop that Maze & Frankie Beverly
I'm tryna show up to the family reunion with
someone worth cuffing with
I hope he got a beard so I can make him mad by
twisting it
Care for you like a mother but
Fight with you like a sister
Defend you like a cousin
But... love you like I'm the one
A partner
Someone to experience life with
Mistakes are cool
So someone I can grow with
Only commitment
Is to be a true friend before anything

GYT

|I lose dignity each time I choose to forgive.
But choosing to not give is choosing to not live.
Often I'm stuck.
Love struck.
Giver of life and good vibes
Even if that gift means the end of me
Crawling toward my demise
by
Pourin love all on my enemy.
Raw
More addicting than anything
But the worst part is my addiction may cost my
seeds
A wanna be. Wanna be free.
Looking ahead I never would've saw
My jaw wrapped around the object that he thinks
with
No not his brain
Mind's washed up like the trash in white
supremacy
Used to be my best friend now I call him my
frenemy
His lustful ways will be the end of me.
And still somehow I'll take pride in that.

I was always loyal, always loving, always
giving...but not to myself.
What happened to my dignity?
He says "baby I know I act like I don't know I
have a jewel but trust me when I say all I want is
you." Each time. I accept. No regrets.
I'm Woman. Woman. Woman of 2015.
No integrity.| #JoviTheModest
1 in 32. 1 in 32. 1 in 32 African American
Women will be diagnosed with HIV in her
lifetime... That's several of the beautiful faces I
see walking around my campus. A customer or
two at my job. Sex is fun but this new world ish
got us messed up. Pregnancy ain't the only thing
we have to worry about. Someone to love ain't
the only thing worth caring about. Let's be
conscious. Agape.

GetYourselfTested PrEP

If it's Nippy then Hustle

4am I'm in the west side of pa
My mom said Jovi you need to lose weight
I'm about to be on that sebi plan
Pop up with a good man
momma just wait
Shout out to jas; da muvah nurture
And shout out phoxx and JR they really for the
culture
Like meek said I be getting to the grind all year
When it comes to fending for the underdog I'm a
monster
When it come to work my soul sold
Everyday I see this social justice system cold
I witness how nippy so I hustle

Chamomile

Happy with her tea
She a little honey
but she strong, that's g cups
Personality like a diva
So bossy
Not flossy
doe
Do re me fa so la ti do
That's the sound of Jovi making music with her
soul
She creates
Movements with her sol
Fueled between by so many stories untold
Qualities like Remy Martin
VSOP
Soon as they think she gon' give em cognac
She come with chamomile in her teacup
Raised with brothers
and boy cousins
A REAL woman so
it's never pinkies up

lost or finding

i am becoming OK
with being lost
lost
just means
There is still places to go
Life to be lived
Love to be explored
lost
just means
the Journey is not over

Rescue

TwelveTwentyNine
Ain't no coming into my life and rescuing me. I
am the kind of woman, the kind of being,

That cannot be rescued

I rescue myself

Through connecting with and living Truth

By the grace of God

Only through God's will,

Can one expose me to me.

Only through something ordained and
orchestrated by

Our creator

Can one break the barrier with me

And when the barrier is broken

It's a beautiful thing

I don't ask for anyone to

Carry this burden for me

I ask those who feel it's in their life path

To connect with me

To pray about it

Meditate on it

Ask the tough questions

Live it

I am not the answer

God is the answer

••••

Sometimes our relationships with other beings is
what makes us feel closest to God; we seek for
our purpose, our Creator's love through our
human connections...and when things don't go
how we want them to, we question our

essence...we question the people we love, the decisions we make, and sometimes we question God; though our spirit is forever, God is the only way to our true selves. And because of this, God is our only true rescue. #TwelveTwentyNine #AreYouListening "achieving necessary steps for emotional balance, spiritual awakening and living well/ fully."

Time today

With titties this long, do I look like I got time today?

Recipe of Modesty

Happy pipe
Happy life
Future wife
Fucking right / fuck me right
He told me stay in my place
Aka (ay Kay) sit on his face
cuz he just loves to please me
I say Baby boy don't tease me
Your nose
It goes
Up and down
From my labia to my clit
Make me soak these sheets so I can hop on that
i love when we dickin around
laughing and shit
then you suddenly dick me down
i cant handle you and the bullet
but you still do it
you hold me down
like are YOU yourself fucking gravity?
Merely merely merely merely
soaked from jovi's stream

Substance

If you stayed off that substance, you might have
some sense ••
But I'm not talking about common sense
Or the one your [grand]parents beat in to you
when you weren't listening
I'm talking about
sense of self
Sense of health
Sense of OMG I'm running my body down
Sense of
A damaged vessel is literal hell
Sense of true love
And genuine friends
Sense of life
Without end

Some may think of drugs when I speak on
substance
But
I'm speaking to whatever your demon is
I'm asking that your higher self
Will tap into its natural substance
So you can preserve your shelf life
[come make this aisle your runway]

Buy you some time
Tap into what's
Inside
Do you recognize?
You are the pistachio
In a crowd full of regular nuts
You are the exception
In a room full of compliments that end with but
You are
The alkaline jawn with popping vitals
And still got a gut
And everything else is a distraction
A distraction from you
A distraction from what
Has been fearfully and wonderfully made
I'm saying everybody else is a candle and you
sage
And the sooner you recognize
That the only stage
That truly matters is the one of which you live
out your God given manners
The better you'll breathe
Your balance will clear out that disease
And I ain't talking [about] covid 19
Who you letting fool you?
What rules you?
King.
Queen.

If you stayed off that substance,
You might have some sense
#JoviTheModest
———— written 5/21/2020 1:11AM

It's Mind over Mandingo
And
I guess that's why I stay single
Jovi Baby
Truly an around the way girl
But
They ain't gon treat me like I'm a stone
When I'm a pearl
Plus Size is a Must Size
So it's a
Plus Queen
Just Queen
Trust Queen
Dey'ain't all mean
Just average
Everybody wanna be ya baby
Tell em hold the carriage
We wait for marriage
Or somethin' like that
They look to you like you Kim K
But you ole school like [you' like] Paris
You so poppin'
Like
Who's ya parents?
A lady that fosters
Lead with my heart so I make decisions without
calculating costs
And

I'm so iconic
So I like comics
Like Jemaine
Not dupri but jones
And shout out to all the men that have shown me
love back home
J Aaron he gon change the world
And shout out to Dris
You gon fuck around and give me a little girl
And
Life is Ruff but you always manage to speak to
my soul
And
Kev that 25th birthday meant everything to me
You and the world may never know
And Qur'an
you such a distinguished man, the world should
call you Don
And can't not shout out my hype man sherm
And shout out to my little sister
2010 she made her world debut
If I teach her anything it's
Women and girls deserve to always feel cute
And
To herself to stay true
And
Don't let no one district you from You
Cuz

You are divinely created with all you will ever
need; your Creator is the truth
And
Shout out to the troops
I ain't talking 'bout the military
But everybody who show you love
when the masses' [act] scary
The ones that show you love all year long
Not just February
I'm getting ahead of myself
Starting to feel like a leap year
It's just I can't stop going when I feel like I got
the heat here
So ima wrap it up
Like it's left overs
Wyclef said gon til November but I think I'll see
y'all October

Jov

aMUSEment

I'm no longer accepting the narrative that black women have to be 10x as great or excellent or "respectable" to reach goals, surpass milestones and have opportunities...or a better quality of life. I understand this expectation is a reality and result of racism (often internalized), misogynistic projections, self-inadequacy and fear. If I'm in a space where thriving in my full essence is viewed as unacceptable then that space ain't for me. Respectfully!

.

.

.

If you've ever struggled with living in truth or being assertive and you've been taking a stand, I totally identify with you and I support you as you continue to do life. When something doesn't sit right with you, write it down! When someone crosses you, write it down! When you have realizations, whether "positive" or "negative", write it down. Write it down in a journal, in a planner, in your phone notes— this will allow you to keep a track

record of people's actions and then hold
yourself and them accountable.
Spiritually, Personally, Professionally,
Physically, Financially and in all aspects of
life, you deserve to be the best you…
w a l k in it, b a s k in it!
#PersonalBoardOfDirectors #Jovi
#Accountability #Assertiveness #Passive
#Aggressive #Communication #TheLevelUp
#TheLevelUpRequiresYouToMoveDifferently
#GodsChild #Women #BlackWomen #LadyBoss
#ImAMuseNotAMule #Dahomey
#DahomeyInMyBlood